THE IRRESPONSIBLES

ARCHIBALD MACLEISH

THE

IRRESPONSIBLES

A Declaration

DUELL, SLOAN AND PEARCE
NEW YORK

first edition

PRINTED IN THE UNITED STATES OF AMERICA

BY QUINN & BODEN COMPANY, INC., RAHWAY, N. J.

THE IRRESPONSIBLES

HISTORY—if honest history continues to be written—will have one question to ask of our generation, people like ourselves. It will be asked of the books we have written, the carbon copies of our correspondence, the photographs of our faces, the minutes of our meetings in the famous rooms before the portraits of our spiritual begetters. The question will be this: Why did the scholars and the writers of our generation in this country, witnesses as they were to the destruction of writing and of scholarship in great areas of Europe and to the exile and the imprisonment and murder of men whose crime was scholarship and writing—witnesses also to the rise in their own country of the same destructive forces with the same impulses, the same motives, the same means—why did the scholars and the writers of our generation in America fail to oppose those forces while they could—while there

3

was still time and still place to oppose them with the arms of scholarship and writing?

It is a question the historians will ask with interest—the gentle, detached, not altogether loving interest with which historians have always questioned the impotent spirits of the dead. Young men working in the paper rubbish of our lives, the old journals, the marginal notations, the printed works, will discover (or so they will think) that the scholars and the writers of our generation in this country had been warned of danger as men were rarely warned before. They will discover (or so they will think) that the common inherited culture of the West, by which alone our scholars and our writers lived, had been attacked in other countries with a stated and explicit purpose to destroy. They will discover that that purpose had been realized. They will discover that a similar purpose backed by similar forces, created by similar conditions, was forming here. And it will seem to them strange—ironical and strange—that the great mass of American

4

scholars and American writers made no effort to defend either themselves or the world by which they lived.

They will make of course the necessary reservations. They will note that societies of scholars and associations of writers adopted resolutions declaring their devotion to civilization. They will note that certain young novelists and poets, the most generous and gallant of their time, unable to endure the outrage and injustice, gave up their lives as writers and enlisted in the hopeless armies to fight brutality with force. But of those who truly faced this danger not with their bodies but their minds, of those who fought the enemies of the intellect with the weapons of the intellect, devoting to that warfare all the strength, all the imagination, all the resources of courage and inventiveness, all the watchfulness by day and night, all the last reserves of hope and skill and pain which men must use whose lives and more than lives are put in danger—of those who fought this danger with the weapons by which this danger could be overcome, they will record the names of very few. And they will ask their question. Why did we, scholars and writers in America in this time, we who had been warned of our danger not only by explicit threats but by explicit action, why did we not fight this danger while the weapons we used best—the weapons of ideas and words—could still be used against it?

It is not a question for which we are altogether unprepared. We have been writing out our answer for many years now in action and inaction, in words and in silence—in learned articles in the scientific journals and in controversial articles in the general magazines, in blank faces after the passionate words, in bored eyes refusing to believe. The answer we have prepared, the answer we have written out for history to find, is the answer Leonardo is said to have given Michelangelo when Michelangelo blamed him for his indifference to the misfortunes of the Florentines. It is the answer of our kind at many other times and places. "Indeed," said Leonardo, "indeed the study of beauty has occupied my whole heart." The study of beauty, the study of history, the study of science, has occupied our whole hearts and the misfortunes of our generation are none of our concern. They are the practical and political concern of practical and political men but the concern of the scholar, the concern of the artist, is with other, purer, more enduring things.

This is the answer we have written down for history to find. I doubt whether it will satisfy the ironic men who come to plague us on that waterfront where Teresias was made to drink the blood and answer. I think indeed it will not satisfy them. For it has not satisfied ourselves. We say with great firmness and authority, speaking by our words and by our silence, that the misfortunes of our generation are economic and political misfortunes from which the scholar can safely hold himself apart. We say this with all the authority of the political scientists of the past to whom the misfortunes of the people were always political and economic and of no concern to the poet, the pure scholar, the artist intent upon his art. We say it also with the authority of the political scientists of the present to whom all phenomena of whatever kind are, by hypothesis, economic and political. But though we say it we do not believe it. For we have observed these misfortunes. They have been acted out for us to see. And what we have seen is this: that the misfortunes of our time are not the misfortunes the philosophers, the theorists, the political scientists have described to us. They are not the practical concern of the practical man and therefore matters of indifference to the scholar. On the contrary, it is the practical man and the practical man alone—the man whose only care is for his belly and his roof—who can safely be indifferent to these troubles. The things he lives by are not menaced. And it is precisely the scholar, the poet—the man whose care is for the structures of the intellect, the houses of the mind—whose heart is caught. For it is the scholar's goods which are in danger.

It is perhaps because we have seen this and yet refuse to see it—because we know one thing and yet continue to declare another—that our minds are so confused and our counsels so bewildering. Nothing is more characteristic of the intellectuals of our generation than their failure to understand what it is that is happening to their world. And nothing explains that failure as precisely as their unwillingness to see what they have seen and to know what they do truly know. They have seen the crisis of their time—they have seen it spelled out, played out, fought out as few observers ever before in history saw the tragedy exposed. They know its ending. And yet they continue to pretend that they do not know. They continue to speak of the crisis of their time as though the war in Europe were that crisis—and the war, they say, is no concern of theirs. They continue to speak of the crisis as though the imperialistic maneuvers, the struggles for markets, the propaganda in the newspapers and the radio, were the crisis—and the maneuvers of imperialism, the propaganda of the press and the struggles for trade they say are no concern of theirs. And yet they know— they know very well because they have seen— that these things are not the crisis but merely its reflections in the mirrors of action. They know that behind the war, behind the diplomatic gestures, behind the black print on the page and the hysterical voices on the air there is something deeper and more dangerous—more dangerous to *them*. They know that it is a condition of men's minds which has produced these things —a condition which existed and exists not only in Europe but in other parts of the world as well and not least in our own country. And they know that this condition of men's minds is not a practical, a political, phenomenon of no concern to the scholar and the man of thought but something very different.

It is not, for example, a matter of purely practical and political interest that great numbers of men in various parts of the world wish passionately and even violently to give up the long labor of liberty and to surrender their wills and their bodies and even their minds to the will of a leader, so that they may achieve at least the dignity of order, at least the dignity of obedience. It is not a matter of purely practical and political significance that whole nations of men have gladly and willingly released themselves not only from their rights as individuals but from their responsibilities as individuals so that they are no longer compelled to feel or to respect the individual humanity of others—or to feel or to respect the things that individual humanity has, over many centuries, created. It is not a matter of purely practical and political importance that governments which once, whatever they may have practiced, protested a respect for learning and the arts, should now permit themselves to show not only the power but worse, far worse, the *willingness,* the *purpose,* to enslave both learning and the arts. It is not a matter of purely practical and political importance that societies which once made part of the community of Western culture should now attempt by murder and outrage and exile to root out that culture and to replace it with private and parochial sciences and private and parochial arts so that frontiers are armed, for the first time in the history of the West, not only along the rivers and the mountains and the boundaries of nations, but across the common earth of culture, the free land that was never fenced before.

I think no honest man will say that these are matters of practical and political significance alone. I think any man who considers with coolness, and without the preconceptions of the dogmas, the character of the crisis of his time will admit, because he will have no choice but to admit, that this crisis is in essence a cultural crisis—a revolt of certain classes, certain conditions of men against the inherited culture of the West and against all common culture—a revolt by no means limited to those nations alone where it has been successful. Wars we have had before—many wars; murder also: inquisition of scholars: torture of askers: suppression and mutilation of truth. But in the past these things have been done, however hypocritically, in the name of truth, in the name of humanity—even in the name of God. The forms of culture were preserved—and in the preservation of a civilization as in the preservation of an art the forms are everything. What is new and unexampled in the times we live in is *the repudiation of the forms.* What is new is a cynical brutality which considers moral self-justification unnecessary and therefore—and this is perhaps its worst indecency—dispenses even with the filthy garment of the hypocrite. To use brutality and force, not in the name of Right nor in the name of God, but in the name of force alone, is to destroy the self-respect and therefore the dignity of the individual life without which the existence of art or learning is inconceivable. To lie, not in the name of truth, but in the name of lies, is to destroy the common basis of communication without which a common culture cannot exist and a work of learning or of art becomes unintelligible.

13

The truth is—the plain and simple truth of which we have so many painful evidences—that the disorder of our time, whatever else it may now be or may become, is in its essentials a revolt against the common culture of the West. For against what but the common culture did this disorder continue to struggle in Germany long after it had overthrown the former state? There was no domestic danger for it to fear. Against what but the Western respect for the dignity of the individual was aimed the long series of outrages against the Jews? The Jews were impotent when they were subjected to the worst abuses. Against what but the Western respect for the common, the nationless, creation of the artist was aimed the destruction of the work of men like Thomas Mann? Thomas Mann had already been repudiated by his people when they accepted the government of his enemies. Against what but the Western belief in the wholeness of Western civilization was aimed the assault upon a church which was no longer a danger to any ruler and the fabrication of a paganism which needed only the blond sopranos on the ends of wires to be Wagner at his worst?

Intellectuals in America and elsewhere—writers, scientists, the men of learning—have attempted to ignore these questions. They have pretended to themselves that the burning of books, the exiling of artists, the invention of mythologies were merely incidents—afterthoughts—decorations: that the true crisis was the crisis of food, the crisis of arms, the crisis created by political forces, by economic collapse,—that they had, and needed have, no truck with it. They have been wrong. These things are not incidents. They are not afterthoughts. They are the essential nature of the revolution of our age. For without this attack upon the habits of the mind, the reliances of the spirit, that revolution could not, by any possibility, have succeeded.

The revolution of our age—the revolution which has finally emerged and declared itself in action—is not the great revolution of the masses

15

of which generous men once dreamed: and which other and less generous men have now so meanly and so bloodily betrayed. The revolution of the masses was a revolution which proposed to set up one faith against another faith, one culture against another culture: a faith in man, a faith in the power of the patterns of men's lives, against a faith in institutions and in money; a culture of the people against a culture of the exploiters of the people. The revolution which has finally and successfully emerged in action has no such faith and no such culture.

It is a revolution of negatives, a revolution of the defeated, a revolution of the dispossessed, a revolution of despair. It is a revolution created out of misery by dread of yet more misery, a revolution created out of disorder by terror of disorder. It is a revolution of gangs, a revolution *against*. And the enemy it is against, the enemy it must destroy, is the enemy which, in all times and in all civilizations, has stood against the revolutions of the gangs—the rule of moral law, the rule of spiritual authority, the rule of intellectual truth. To establish the negative revolutions, the revolutions of which the only aim is power, the revolutions which have no means but force, it is necessary first to destroy the authority of the unseen sayings of the mind. It is necessary to destroy the things the mind has made. Caliban in the miserable and besotted swamp is the symbol of this revolution. As long as the unseen beauty in the air retains its voices and its seductive music and its stinging whips the revolutions of the gangs are clumsy, blundering, grotesque and foolish. They can bellow and threaten and boast and gesture with their arms but in the end the invisible voices of the air, the invisible power of the ideal will master them. They have one hope of success and only one—the destruction of the whole system of ideas, the whole respect for truth, the whole authority of excellence which places law above force, beauty above cruelty, singleness above numbers.

It is the distinction of our time—perhaps unhappily its most memorable distinction—that it and it alone has provided the formula by which this overthrow could be achieved. Only in our time has the revolution of the gangs discovered a strategy and a leadership brutal enough, cynical enough, cunning enough to destroy the entire authority of the inherited culture and thereafter to seal the doors against the searching and the asking of the scholar's mind, the artist's mind, so that the revolution of force, the revolution of despair could flower and fulfill its possibilities. Only in our time has the revolution of the gangs shown itself openly and admittedly as the thing it is—a revolution of cruelty, cunning and despair against the authority and the discipline of the mind.

It is to this disorder and not to some political and partisan dissension, not to some accidental economic breakdown—practical and political matters for the men of politics and practice—it is to this direct, explicit and intentional attack upon the scholar's world and the scholar's life and the

18

scholar's work that American scholarship has been indifferent. Or if not indifferent, then inactive, merely watchful—fearful, watchful and inactive. And it is there that history will place its questions.

How could we sit back as spectators of a war against ourselves?

Did we suppose the newly discovered techniques of deception, of falsehood as a military force, of strategic fraud, were incapable of reaching us—incapable of crossing sea water? We had seen their methods drive their conquests through the countries of the world more rapidly than Alexander or Napoleon or Tamerlane or any other conqueror or killer.

Or was it something else we thought? Did we believe others would defend us? Did we think the issue was an issue of strategy, an issue of battles? Did we think the British and the French would win their war and so defend us? But we knew very well, because we had seen, that this war was not a war fought in the open on the military

19

front, but a war fought in the back street and the dark stair—a war fought within the city, within the house, within the mind—a war of treason: a war of corruption: a war of lies. And against treason and corruption and lies, battle fleets and grand armies are impotent.

The questions answer themselves and yet provide no answer. For if we did not believe we were safe by sea water, or if we did not believe others would save us, then our failure to act in our own defense becomes a curious thing. What has prevented us from acting? Lack of courage? It is difficult to indict a generation for lack of courage. Lack of wisdom? There is wisdom enough in other matters.

I think, speaking only of what I have seen myself and heard—I think it is neither lack of courage nor lack of wisdom, but a different reason which has prevented our generation of intellectuals in this country from acting in their own defense. I think it is the organization of the intellectual life of our time. Specifically, I think it is the division and therefore the destruction of intellectual responsibility. The men of intellectual duty, those who should have been responsible for action, have divided themselves into two castes, two cults—the scholars and the writers. Neither accepts responsibility for the common culture or for its defense.

There was a time a century ago, two centuries ago, when men who practiced our professions would have accepted this responsibility without an instant's hesitation. A century ago the professions of the writer and the scholar were united in the single profession of the man of letters and the man of letters was responsible in everything that touched the mind. He was a man of wholeness of purpose, of singleness of intention—a single intellectual champion, admittedly responsible for the defense of the inherited tradition, avowedly partisan of its practice. Where those who practice our several professions divide the learned world and the creative world between them in irresponsible and neutral states, the man of letters inhabited both learning and the world of letters like an empire.

He was a man of learning whose learning was employed not for its own sake in a kind of academic narcissism but for the sake of decent living in his time. He was a writer whose writing was used not to mirror an abstract and unrelated present but to illuminate that present by placing it in just relation to its past. He was therefore and necessarily a man who admitted a responsibility for the survival and vitality of the common and accumulated experience of the mind, for this experience was to him the air he breathed, the perspective of his thinking. Learning to him was no plump pigeon carcass to be picked at for his private pleasure and his private fame but a profession practiced for the common good. Writing was not an ornament, a jewel, but a means to ends, a weapon, the most powerful of weapons, a weapon to be used. Whatever threatened learning or the ends of learning challenged the man of letters. Whatever struck at truth or closed off question or defiled an art or violated decency of thinking struck at him. And he struck back with every weapon masters of the word could find to strike with. Milton defending freedom of the mind in sentences which outlive every name of those who struck at freedom, Voltaire displaying naked to the grin of history the tyrants who were great until he made them small, Bartolomé de las Casas gentling cruel priests and brutal captains with the dreadful strokes of truth—Las Casas, Milton and Voltaire were men of letters—men who confessed an obligation to defend the disciplines of thought not in their own but in the general interest.

Had men like these been living in our time— had the intellectuals of our time been whole and loyal—it would, I think, have been impossible for the revolution of the gangs to have succeeded where success has been most dangerous—in the perversion of the judgments of the mind. Murder is not absolved of immorality by committing murder. Murder is absolved of immorality by bring-

23

ing men to think that murder is not evil. This only the perversion of the mind can bring about. And the perversion of the mind is only possible when those who should be heard in its defense are silent.

They are silent in our time because there are no voices which accept responsibility for speaking. Even the unimaginable indecencies of propaganda—even the corruption of the word itself in Germany and Russia and in Spain and elsewhere —even the open triumph of the lie, produced no answer such as Voltaire in his generation would have given. And for this reason—that the man who could have been Voltaire, who could have been Las Casas, does not live: the man of intellectual *office,* the man of intellectual *calling,* the man who *professes* letters—professes an obligation as a servant of the mind to defend the mind's integrity against every physical power—professes an obligation to defend the labors of the mind and the structures it has created and the means by which it lives, not only privately and safely in his

24

study, not only strictly and securely in the controversies of the learned press, but publicly and at the public risk and danger of his life. He does not exist because the man of letters no longer exists. And the man of letters no longer exists because he has been driven from our world and from our time by the division of his kingdom. The single responsibility, the wholeness of function of the man of letters, has been replaced by the divided function, the mutual antagonism, the isolated irresponsibility of two figures, each free of obligation, each separated from a portion of his duty—the scholar and the writer.

Why this substitution has come about—whether because the methods of scientific inquiry, carried over into the humanities, destroyed the loyalties and habits of the mind or for some other reason, I leave to wiser men to say. The point is that there has been a substitution. The country of the man of letters has been divided between his heirs. The country that was once the past and present—the past made useful to the reasons of the present, the present understood against the knowledge of the past—the country that was once the past and present brought together in the mind, is now divided into past on one side, present on the other.

Past is the scholar's country: present is the writer's. The writer sees the present on the faces of the world and leaves the past to rot in its own rubbish. The scholar digs his ivory cellar in the ruins of the past and lets the present sicken as it will. A few exceptions noted here and there—men like Thomas Mann—the gulf between these countries is complete. And the historical novels fashionable at the moment, the vulgarizations of science, the digests of philosophy only define its depth as a plank across a chasm makes the chasm deeper. That it should be necessary to throw such flimsy flights from one side to the other of the learned world shows how deeply and disastrously the split was made.

That scholarship suffers or that writing suffers by the change is not asserted. Scholarship may be more scientific: writing may be purer. Indeed there are many who believe, and I among them, that the time we live in has produced more first-rate writers than any but the very greatest ages, and there are scholars of a scholarship as hard, as honest, as devoted as any we have known. But excellence of scholarship and writing are not now in question. What matters now is the defense of culture—the defense truly, and in the most literal terms, of civilization as men have known it for the last two thousand years. And there the substitution for the man of letters of the scholar and the writer, however pure the scholarship, however excellent the writing, is a tragic and immeasurable loss. For neither the modern scholar nor the modern writer admits responsibility for the defense. They assert on the contrary, each in his particular way, an irresponsibility as complete as it is singular.

The irresponsibility of the scholar is the irresponsibility of the scientist upon whose laboratory insulation he has patterned all his work. The scholar has made himself as indifferent to values, as careless of significance, as bored with meanings as the chemist. He is a refugee from consequences, an exile from the responsibilities of moral choice. He has taught himself to say with the physicist—and with some others whom history remembers—"What is truth?" He has taught himself with the biologist to refrain from judgments of better or worse. His words of praise are the laboratory words—objectivity—detachment—dispassion. His pride is to be scientific, neuter, skeptical, detached—superior to final judgment or absolute belief. In his capacity as scholar the modern scholar does not occupy the present. In his capacity as scholar he loves the word—but only the word which entails no judgments, involves no decisions, accomplishes no actions. Where the man of letters of other centuries domesticated the past within the rustling of the present, making it stand among us like the meaning of a statue among trees, the modern scholar in his capacity as scholar leaves the present and returns across the past where all the men are marble. Where the man of letters of other centuries quarried his learning from the past to build the present the modern scholar quarries his learning from the past to dig the quarries.

It is not for nothing that the modern scholar invented the Ph.D. thesis as his principal contribution to literary form. The Ph.D. thesis is the perfect image of his world. It is work done for the sake of doing work—perfectly conscientious, perfectly laborious, perfectly irresponsible. The modern scholar at his best and worst is both these things—perfectly conscientious, laborious and competent: perfectly irresponsible for the saving of his world. He remembers how in the Civil Wars in England the scholars, devoted only to their proper tasks, founded the Royal Society. He remembers how through other wars and other dangers the scholars kept the lamp of learning lighted. He does not consider that the scholars then did other things as well as trim the lamp wicks. He does not consider either that the dan-

gers change and can be greater. He has his work
to do. He has his book to finish. He hopes the
war will not destroy the manuscripts he works
with. He is the pure, the perfect type of irresponsibility—the man who acts as though the fire
could not burn him because he has no business
with the fire. He knows because he cannot help
but know, reading his papers, talking to his
friends—he knows this fire has consumed the
books, the spirit, everything he lives by, flesh itself—in other countries. He knows this but he
will not know. It's not his business. Whose business is it then? He will not answer even that. He
has his work to do. He has his book to finish . . .

The writer's irresponsibility is of a different
kind. Where the modern scholar escapes from
the adult judgments of the mind by taking the
disinterested man of science as his model, the
modern writer escapes by imitation of the artist.
He practices his writing as a painter does his
painting. He thinks as artist—which is to say
he thinks without responsibility to anything but

truth of feeling. He observes as artist—which is to say that he observes with honesty and truthfulness and without comment. His devotion, as with every honest painter, is devotion to the thing observed, the actual thing, the thing without its consequences or its antecedents, naked of judgment, stripped of causes and effects. The invisible world, the intellectual world, the world of the relation of ideas, the world of judgments, of values, the world in which truth is good and lies are evil—this world has no existence to the honest artist or to the honest writer who takes the artist for his model. His duty is to strip all this away—to strip away the moral preference, the intellectual association.

He sees the world as a god sees it—without morality, without care, without judgment. People look like this. People act like that. He shows them looking, acting. It is not his business why they look so, why they act so. It is enough that he should "make them happen." This is the whole test, the whole criterion, of the work of the writer-artist—to show things as they "really happen": to write with such skill, such penetration of the physical presence of the world, that the action seen, the action described, will "really happen" on his page. If he concerns himself with motive at all he concerns himself with the "real" motive, meaning the discreditable motive which the actor conceals from himself. His most searching purpose is to find, not the truth of human action, but the low-down, the discreditable explanation which excuses him from care. The suggestion that there are things in the world—ideas, conceptions, ways of thinking—which the writer-artist should defend from attack: the suggestion above all that he was under obligation to defend the inherited culture, would strike him as ridiculous.

Artists do not save the world. They practice art. They practice it as Goya practiced it among the cannon in Madrid. And if this war is not Napoleon in Spain but something even worse than that? They practice art. Or they put the art aside and take a rifle and go out and fight. But not *as artists*. The artist does not fight. The artist's obligations are obligations to his art. His responsibility—his one responsibility—is to his art. He has no other. Not even when his art itself, his chance to practice it, his need to live where it is practiced, may be in danger. The writer-artist will write a bloody story about the expense of blood. He will present the face of agony as it has rarely been presented. But not even then will he take the weapon of his words and carry it to the barricades of intellectual warfare, to the storming of belief, the fortifying of conviction where alone this fighting can be won.

There are examples in history of civilizations made impotent by excess of culture. No one, I think, will say of us that we lost our intellectual liberties on this account. But it may well be said, and said with equally ironic emphasis, that the men of thought, the men of learning in this country were deceived and rendered impotent by

33

the best they knew. To the scholar impartiality, objectivity, detachment were ideal qualities he taught himself laboriously and painfully to acquire. To the writer objectivity and detachment were his writer's pride. Both subjected themselves to inconceivable restraints, endless disciplines to reach these ends. And both succeeded. Both writers and scholars freed themselves of the subjective passions, the emotional preconceptions which color conviction and judgment. Both writers and scholars freed themselves of the personal responsibility associated with personal choice. They emerged free, pure and single into the antiseptic air of objectivity. And by that sublimation of the mind they prepared the mind's disaster.

If it is a consolation to the philosophers of earlier civilizations to know that they lost the things they loved because of the purity of their devotion, then perhaps this consolation will be ours as well. I doubt if we will profit by it or receive much praise.

DATE DUE

810.904   229187
M163i

    MacLeish, Archibald
AUTHOR

      The irresponsibles
TITLE

DATE DUE	BORROWER'S NAME

MacLeish   229187